50 Italian Classics Reinvented Recipes

By: Kelly Johnson

Table of Contents

- Cauliflower Crust Margherita Pizza
- Zucchini Noodles with Pesto
- Sweet Potato Gnocchi
- Gluten-Free Lasagna
- Eggplant Parmesan Bites
- Butternut Squash Risotto
- Spaghetti Squash Carbonara
- Grilled Polenta with Mushroom Ragù
- Chicken Piccata with Lemon Cauliflower Rice
- Baked Ravioli with Spinach and Ricotta
- Cauliflower-Crusted Frittata
- Whole Wheat Penne Arrabbiata
- Seared Salmon with Basil Pesto
- Spaghetti with Roasted Garlic and Cherry Tomatoes
- Risotto with Asparagus and Lemon
- Zucchini Lasagna Rolls
- Cucumber Carpaccio with Parmesan
- Shrimp Scampi with Zoodles
- Portobello Mushroom Caprese
- Grilled Eggplant Rollatini
- Pesto-Crusted Chicken
- Ricotta and Spinach Stuffed Chicken Breasts
- Quinoa and Roasted Vegetable Salad
- Spaghetti alla Chitarra with Crab
- Stuffed Artichokes with Lemon and Parmesan
- Fennel and Orange Salad
- Braised Beef with Polenta
- Roasted Garlic and Herb Focaccia
- Baked Ziti with Chicken Sausage
- Pistachio Pesto Pasta
- Cabbage and Sausage Risotto
- Cacciatore with Cauliflower Rice
- Baked Eggplant with Tomato and Basil
- Saffron Risotto with Scallops
- Grilled Shrimp and Zucchini Skewers

- Lemon-Basil Chicken with Spaghetti
- Mushroom and Ricotta Stuffed Shells
- Fettuccine Alfredo with Cauliflower
- Roasted Red Pepper Pappardelle
- Polenta Fries with Marinara Sauce
- Spinach and Ricotta Tortellini
- Lemon and Garlic Roasted Chicken
- Beetroot Ravioli with Goat Cheese
- Pumpkin Risotto with Sage
- Grilled Veal Milanese
- Spinach and Mushroom Stuffed Peppers
- Roasted Tomato and Basil Soup
- Baked Parmesan-Crusted Zucchini
- Tuna Puttanesca
- Gnocchi with Brown Butter Sage Sauce

Cauliflower Crust Margherita Pizza

Ingredients:

- **1 medium cauliflower**, riced
- **1 egg**
- **1 cup shredded mozzarella cheese**
- **1/4 cup grated Parmesan cheese**
- **1/2 teaspoon garlic powder**
- **1/2 teaspoon dried oregano**
- **Salt and pepper**, to taste
- **1/2 cup pizza sauce**
- **1 cup fresh mozzarella balls**, sliced
- **Fresh basil leaves**, for garnish
- **Olive oil**, for drizzling

Instructions:

1. Preheat the oven to 400°F (200°C). Line a baking sheet with parchment paper.
2. Rice the cauliflower using a food processor, then microwave it in a bowl for 5-7 minutes. Allow it to cool, then wring out excess moisture using a clean towel.
3. In a bowl, mix the cauliflower, egg, mozzarella, Parmesan, garlic powder, oregano, salt, and pepper.
4. Shape the cauliflower mixture into a pizza crust on the prepared baking sheet. Bake for 15-20 minutes until golden and firm.
5. Remove from the oven, spread pizza sauce on top, and arrange fresh mozzarella slices.
6. Return to the oven for another 5-7 minutes until cheese is melted and bubbly.
7. Garnish with fresh basil leaves and drizzle with olive oil before serving.

Zucchini Noodles with Pesto

Ingredients:

- **2 medium zucchinis**, spiralized
- **1/4 cup pesto sauce** (store-bought or homemade)
- **1 tablespoon olive oil**
- **1/4 cup cherry tomatoes**, halved
- **Parmesan cheese**, for garnish

Instructions:

1. Heat olive oil in a large skillet over medium heat. Add zucchini noodles and sauté for 3-4 minutes until tender but still firm.
2. Remove from heat and toss the zucchini noodles with pesto sauce.
3. Garnish with cherry tomatoes and Parmesan cheese before serving.

Sweet Potato Gnocchi

Ingredients:

- 2 medium sweet potatoes
- 1 egg
- 1 1/2 cups gluten-free flour
- 1/2 teaspoon salt
- 1/4 teaspoon nutmeg

Instructions:

1. Preheat the oven to 400°F (200°C). Pierce the sweet potatoes with a fork and bake for 45-60 minutes until tender.
2. Once cooled, scoop the flesh from the sweet potatoes and mash it.
3. In a bowl, combine the mashed sweet potatoes, egg, flour, salt, and nutmeg. Mix until a dough forms.
4. Roll the dough into ropes and cut into small pieces. Press each piece with a fork to create the gnocchi shape.
5. Boil a large pot of salted water, then drop the gnocchi in batches. Cook for 2-3 minutes or until they float to the surface. Remove with a slotted spoon.
6. Serve with a sauce of your choice, such as brown butter or marinara.

Gluten-Free Lasagna

Ingredients:

- 9 gluten-free lasagna noodles
- 1 lb ground beef or turkey
- 1 onion, chopped
- 2 cloves garlic, minced
- 1 jar marinara sauce
- 2 cups ricotta cheese
- 2 cups shredded mozzarella cheese
- 1/2 cup grated Parmesan cheese
- 1 egg
- 2 teaspoons dried oregano
- Salt and pepper, to taste

Instructions:

1. Cook the lasagna noodles according to package instructions. Drain and set aside.
2. In a skillet, cook the ground meat with onion and garlic over medium heat until browned. Drain any excess fat.
3. Stir in the marinara sauce and oregano, and season with salt and pepper. Simmer for 10 minutes.
4. In a bowl, mix ricotta cheese, egg, mozzarella, and Parmesan.
5. Preheat the oven to 375°F (190°C). In a baking dish, layer the ingredients: start with a layer of meat sauce, then noodles, followed by the ricotta mixture. Repeat layers until all ingredients are used.
6. Top with mozzarella and Parmesan. Cover with foil and bake for 25-30 minutes, then remove the foil and bake for an additional 10 minutes until the cheese is bubbly and golden.

Eggplant Parmesan Bites

Ingredients:

- **2 medium eggplants,** sliced into 1/2-inch rounds
- **1 cup gluten-free breadcrumbs**
- **1/2 cup grated Parmesan cheese**
- **1 egg**
- **1 cup marinara sauce**
- **Olive oil**, for frying

Instructions:

1. Preheat the oven to 400°F (200°C) and line a baking sheet with parchment paper.
2. Dip each eggplant slice into the egg, then coat with a mixture of breadcrumbs and Parmesan cheese.
3. Heat olive oil in a skillet over medium-high heat. Fry the eggplant slices for 2-3 minutes per side until golden brown.
4. Arrange the fried eggplant slices on the baking sheet and bake for 10 minutes.
5. Serve with marinara sauce for dipping.

Butternut Squash Risotto

Ingredients:

- **1 small butternut squash**, peeled and diced
- **1 tablespoon olive oil**
- **1 onion**, chopped
- **2 cloves garlic**, minced
- **1 1/2 cups Arborio rice**
- **4 cups vegetable broth**
- **1/2 cup white wine**
- **1/4 cup grated Parmesan cheese**
- **Salt and pepper**, to taste

Instructions:

1. Preheat the oven to 400°F (200°C). Toss butternut squash cubes with olive oil, salt, and pepper. Roast for 20-25 minutes until tender.
2. In a large skillet, heat olive oil over medium heat. Add onion and garlic, cooking until softened.
3. Stir in the rice and cook for 1-2 minutes, allowing it to lightly toast.
4. Gradually add the wine and broth, one ladle at a time, stirring continuously. Allow the liquid to absorb before adding more.
5. Once the rice is cooked through, stir in the roasted butternut squash and Parmesan cheese. Adjust seasoning with salt and pepper.

Spaghetti Squash Carbonara

Ingredients:

- **1 medium spaghetti squash**
- **2 tablespoons olive oil**
- **4 slices bacon**, chopped
- **2 eggs**
- **1/2 cup grated Parmesan cheese**
- **Salt and pepper**, to taste

Instructions:

1. Preheat the oven to 400°F (200°C). Cut the spaghetti squash in half, remove the seeds, and drizzle with olive oil. Roast for 40-45 minutes until tender.
2. While the squash is roasting, cook the bacon in a skillet until crispy. Remove from the skillet and set aside.
3. In a bowl, whisk together the eggs, Parmesan cheese, salt, and pepper.
4. Once the squash is done, use a fork to scrape the flesh into spaghetti-like strands.
5. Toss the spaghetti squash with the bacon and egg mixture, allowing the heat from the squash to cook the eggs and create a creamy sauce.
6. Serve with extra Parmesan and black pepper.

Grilled Polenta with Mushroom Ragù

Ingredients:

- **1 tube polenta**, sliced into 1/2-inch rounds
- **1 tablespoon olive oil**
- **2 cups mushrooms**, sliced
- **1/2 onion**, chopped
- **2 cloves garlic**, minced
- **1/2 cup vegetable broth**
- **1 tablespoon balsamic vinegar**
- **1 teaspoon thyme**
- **Salt and pepper**, to taste

Instructions:

1. Preheat the grill to medium-high heat. Brush the polenta rounds with olive oil and grill for 3-4 minutes on each side until crispy.
2. In a skillet, sauté the onions and garlic in olive oil until softened. Add the mushrooms and cook until browned.
3. Stir in the vegetable broth, balsamic vinegar, and thyme. Simmer for 5-7 minutes, reducing the sauce.
4. Serve the grilled polenta topped with the mushroom ragù.

Chicken Piccata with Lemon Cauliflower Rice

Ingredients:

- 4 boneless, skinless chicken breasts
- 1/4 cup gluten-free flour
- 2 tablespoons olive oil
- 1/4 cup lemon juice
- 1/2 cup chicken broth
- 1 tablespoon capers
- **1 head cauliflower**, grated into rice-sized pieces
- **Salt and pepper**, to taste

Instructions:

1. Season the chicken breasts with salt and pepper, then dredge in flour.
2. Heat olive oil in a skillet over medium-high heat. Cook the chicken for 4-5 minutes per side until golden and cooked through. Remove from the skillet and set aside.
3. In the same skillet, add lemon juice, chicken broth, and capers. Simmer for 2-3 minutes.
4. While the sauce simmers, sauté the grated cauliflower in a separate skillet with olive oil, salt, and pepper for 5-7 minutes until tender.
5. Serve the chicken with the lemon sauce and cauliflower rice.

Baked Ravioli with Spinach and Ricotta

Ingredients:

- **1 package cheese ravioli** (fresh or frozen)
- **1 cup ricotta cheese**
- **1 cup fresh spinach**, chopped
- **2 cups marinara sauce**
- **1 cup shredded mozzarella cheese**
- **1/4 cup grated Parmesan cheese**
- **1 teaspoon Italian seasoning**

Instructions:

1. Preheat the oven to 375°F (190°C). Lightly grease a baking dish.
2. Cook the ravioli according to package instructions and drain.
3. In a bowl, mix ricotta, spinach, Parmesan, and Italian seasoning.
4. Spread a layer of marinara sauce in the baking dish, then layer with ravioli, ricotta mixture, and mozzarella. Repeat layers, finishing with mozzarella on top.
5. Cover with foil and bake for 20 minutes. Remove foil and bake for an additional 10 minutes until the cheese is bubbly and golden.

Cauliflower-Crusted Frittata

Ingredients:

- **1 medium cauliflower**, riced
- **6 eggs**
- **1/2 cup shredded cheese** (cheddar or mozzarella)
- **1 cup mixed vegetables** (e.g., bell peppers, onions, and spinach)
- **1/4 cup milk**
- **Salt and pepper**, to taste

Instructions:

1. Preheat the oven to 375°F (190°C). Grease a pie dish or oven-safe skillet.
2. Cook the riced cauliflower in a skillet over medium heat until softened. Spread it evenly in the dish as a base.
3. In a bowl, whisk eggs, milk, salt, and pepper. Stir in cheese and vegetables.
4. Pour the egg mixture over the cauliflower base. Bake for 20-25 minutes until set and golden on top.

Whole Wheat Penne Arrabbiata

Ingredients:

- **12 oz whole wheat penne**
- **2 tablespoons olive oil**
- **3 cloves garlic**, minced
- **1/2 teaspoon red pepper flakes**
- **1 can (14 oz) crushed tomatoes**
- **1 teaspoon dried oregano**
- **Salt and pepper**, to taste
- **Fresh basil leaves**, for garnish

Instructions:

1. Cook the penne according to package instructions. Drain and set aside.
2. In a skillet, heat olive oil over medium heat. Sauté garlic and red pepper flakes until fragrant.
3. Add crushed tomatoes, oregano, salt, and pepper. Simmer for 10 minutes.
4. Toss the penne with the sauce and garnish with fresh basil.

Seared Salmon with Basil Pesto

Ingredients:

- **4 salmon fillets**
- **2 tablespoons olive oil**
- **1/2 cup basil pesto** (store-bought or homemade)
- **Salt and pepper**, to taste
- **Lemon wedges**, for serving

Instructions:

1. Heat olive oil in a skillet over medium-high heat. Season salmon with salt and pepper.
2. Sear the salmon for 4-5 minutes per side until golden and cooked through.
3. Serve with a dollop of basil pesto and a squeeze of lemon juice.

Spaghetti with Roasted Garlic and Cherry Tomatoes

Ingredients:

- **12 oz spaghetti**
- **1 pint cherry tomatoes**
- **1 head garlic**
- **2 tablespoons olive oil**
- **1/4 cup grated Parmesan cheese**
- **Salt and pepper**, to taste
- **Fresh basil**, for garnish

Instructions:

1. Preheat the oven to 400°F (200°C). Slice the top off the garlic head, drizzle with olive oil, and wrap in foil. Roast for 25-30 minutes.
2. Toss cherry tomatoes with olive oil, salt, and pepper. Spread on a baking sheet and roast alongside the garlic until blistered.
3. Cook spaghetti according to package instructions. Drain and set aside.
4. Squeeze the roasted garlic cloves into the spaghetti and toss with tomatoes, olive oil, Parmesan, and fresh basil.

Risotto with Asparagus and Lemon

Ingredients:

- **1 cup Arborio rice**
- **4 cups vegetable broth**, warmed
- **1 tablespoon olive oil**
- **1/2 onion**, finely chopped
- **1 cup asparagus**, chopped
- **1/4 cup grated Parmesan cheese**
- **1 tablespoon lemon juice**
- **Zest of 1 lemon**
- **Salt and pepper**, to taste

Instructions:

1. In a skillet, heat olive oil and sauté onions until translucent. Add rice and toast for 1-2 minutes.
2. Gradually add warm broth, one ladle at a time, stirring continuously until absorbed.
3. When the rice is nearly done, stir in asparagus and cook until tender.
4. Add Parmesan, lemon juice, and zest. Adjust seasoning and serve warm.

Zucchini Lasagna Rolls

Ingredients:

- **2 medium zucchinis**, thinly sliced lengthwise
- **1 cup ricotta cheese**
- **1/2 cup shredded mozzarella cheese**
- **1/4 cup grated Parmesan cheese**
- **1 cup marinara sauce**
- **1 teaspoon Italian seasoning**
- **Salt and pepper**, to taste

Instructions:

1. Preheat the oven to 375°F (190°C). Spread marinara sauce in a baking dish.
2. Mix ricotta, mozzarella, Parmesan, Italian seasoning, salt, and pepper in a bowl.
3. Spread the ricotta mixture on each zucchini slice and roll tightly. Place rolls seam-side down in the dish.
4. Bake for 20-25 minutes until bubbly and golden on top.

Cucumber Carpaccio with Parmesan

Ingredients:

- **2 cucumbers**, thinly sliced
- **2 tablespoons olive oil**
- **1 tablespoon lemon juice**
- **1/4 cup shaved Parmesan cheese**
- **Salt and pepper**, to taste
- **Fresh dill**, for garnish

Instructions:

1. Arrange cucumber slices on a serving plate.
2. Drizzle with olive oil and lemon juice. Sprinkle with Parmesan, salt, and pepper.
3. Garnish with fresh dill before serving.

Shrimp Scampi with Zoodles

Ingredients:

- **2 medium zucchinis**, spiralized
- **1 lb shrimp**, peeled and deveined
- **3 cloves garlic**, minced
- **2 tablespoons olive oil**
- **1/4 cup white wine**
- **Juice of 1 lemon**
- **1/4 cup grated Parmesan cheese**
- **Salt and pepper**, to taste

Instructions:

1. Heat olive oil in a skillet over medium heat. Sauté garlic until fragrant, then add shrimp and cook until pink.
2. Add white wine and lemon juice. Simmer for 2-3 minutes.
3. Toss the zoodles with the shrimp mixture, cooking for 1-2 minutes until tender.
4. Sprinkle with Parmesan and serve warm.

Portobello Mushroom Caprese

Ingredients:

- **4 large Portobello mushrooms**, stems removed
- **2 medium tomatoes**, sliced
- **4 slices fresh mozzarella**
- **2 tablespoons balsamic glaze**
- **1 tablespoon olive oil**
- **Fresh basil leaves**
- **Salt and pepper**, to taste

Instructions:

1. Preheat oven to 400°F (200°C). Brush the mushrooms with olive oil and season with salt and pepper.
2. Place mushrooms on a baking sheet, gill-side up, and roast for 10 minutes.
3. Remove from oven and layer each mushroom with tomato slices and mozzarella.
4. Return to the oven for 5-7 minutes, or until the cheese melts.
5. Drizzle with balsamic glaze and garnish with fresh basil before serving.

Grilled Eggplant Rollatini

Ingredients:

- **2 large eggplants**, sliced lengthwise
- **1 cup ricotta cheese**
- **1/4 cup grated Parmesan cheese**
- **1 cup marinara sauce**
- **1/2 cup shredded mozzarella cheese**
- **1 teaspoon Italian seasoning**
- **Salt and pepper**, to taste

Instructions:

1. Preheat a grill or grill pan. Season eggplant slices with salt and pepper, then grill until tender.
2. Mix ricotta, Parmesan, Italian seasoning, salt, and pepper in a bowl.
3. Spread a layer of the ricotta mixture on each eggplant slice and roll tightly.
4. Place rolls in a baking dish, top with marinara and mozzarella, and bake at 375°F (190°C) for 15-20 minutes.

Pesto-Crusted Chicken

Ingredients:

- **4 chicken breasts**
- **1/2 cup basil pesto**
- **1/4 cup panko breadcrumbs**
- **2 tablespoons grated Parmesan cheese**
- **Salt and pepper**, to taste

Instructions:

1. Preheat oven to 400°F (200°C). Season chicken breasts with salt and pepper.
2. Spread pesto over each chicken breast.
3. Mix breadcrumbs and Parmesan, then sprinkle over the pesto layer.
4. Place chicken on a baking sheet and bake for 20-25 minutes, or until fully cooked.

Ricotta and Spinach Stuffed Chicken Breasts

Ingredients:

- **4 chicken breasts**
- **1 cup fresh spinach**, chopped
- **1/2 cup ricotta cheese**
- **1/4 cup shredded mozzarella cheese**
- **Salt and pepper**, to taste

Instructions:

1. Preheat oven to 375°F (190°C). Butterfly the chicken breasts and season with salt and pepper.
2. Mix spinach, ricotta, and mozzarella in a bowl.
3. Stuff each chicken breast with the ricotta mixture and secure with toothpicks.
4. Bake for 25-30 minutes, or until chicken is fully cooked.

Quinoa and Roasted Vegetable Salad

Ingredients:

- **1 cup quinoa**, cooked
- **1 cup cherry tomatoes**, halved
- **1 zucchini**, diced
- **1 red bell pepper**, diced
- **2 tablespoons olive oil**
- **1 tablespoon balsamic vinegar**
- **Salt and pepper**, to taste

Instructions:

1. Preheat oven to 400°F (200°C). Toss zucchini, bell pepper, and cherry tomatoes with olive oil, salt, and pepper. Roast for 15-20 minutes.
2. Combine cooked quinoa and roasted vegetables in a bowl.
3. Drizzle with balsamic vinegar, toss well, and serve warm or chilled.

Spaghetti alla Chitarra with Crab

Ingredients:

- **12 oz spaghetti alla chitarra**
- **1 cup crab meat**
- **3 cloves garlic**, minced
- **2 tablespoons olive oil**
- **1/4 cup white wine**
- **Juice of 1 lemon**
- **Salt and pepper**, to taste
- **Fresh parsley**, chopped

Instructions:

1. Cook the spaghetti according to package instructions. Reserve 1/4 cup pasta water.
2. Heat olive oil in a skillet and sauté garlic until fragrant.
3. Add crab meat, white wine, and lemon juice. Simmer for 3-4 minutes.
4. Toss spaghetti with the crab mixture, adding reserved pasta water if needed.
5. Garnish with parsley and serve.

Stuffed Artichokes with Lemon and Parmesan

Ingredients:

- 4 large artichokes
- 1 cup breadcrumbs
- 1/4 cup grated Parmesan cheese
- 2 cloves garlic, minced
- Zest of 1 lemon
- 2 tablespoons olive oil

Instructions:

1. Trim and prepare artichokes for stuffing. Steam them for 15-20 minutes until slightly tender.
2. Mix breadcrumbs, Parmesan, garlic, lemon zest, and olive oil.
3. Stuff each artichoke with the breadcrumb mixture.
4. Bake at 375°F (190°C) for 20-25 minutes until golden and tender.

Fennel and Orange Salad

Ingredients:

- **2 fennel bulbs**, thinly sliced
- **2 oranges**, segmented
- **1 tablespoon olive oil**
- **1 tablespoon lemon juice**
- **Salt and pepper**, to taste
- **Fresh parsley**, for garnish

Instructions:

1. Arrange fennel slices and orange segments on a plate.
2. Drizzle with olive oil and lemon juice. Season with salt and pepper.
3. Garnish with fresh parsley and serve chilled.

Braised Beef with Polenta

Ingredients:

- **2 lbs beef chuck**, cut into chunks
- **1 onion**, diced
- **3 cloves garlic**, minced
- **2 cups beef broth**
- **1 cup red wine**
- **2 cups polenta**, cooked
- **1 tablespoon olive oil**
- **Salt and pepper**, to taste

Instructions:

1. Heat olive oil in a Dutch oven and brown beef chunks on all sides. Remove and set aside.
2. Sauté onions and garlic until softened. Add beef, broth, and wine.
3. Cover and braise in a 325°F (160°C) oven for 2-3 hours until tender.
4. Serve over creamy polenta.

Roasted Garlic and Herb Focaccia

Ingredients:

- **3 1/2 cups all-purpose flour**
- **1 packet (2 1/4 tsp) active dry yeast**
- **1 cup warm water**
- **1/4 cup olive oil**, plus more for drizzling
- **3 cloves roasted garlic**, mashed
- **1 tablespoon fresh rosemary**, chopped
- **1 teaspoon salt**
- **Sea salt flakes**, for garnish

Instructions:

1. In a bowl, mix warm water and yeast. Let it sit for 5 minutes until foamy.
2. Add flour, olive oil, roasted garlic, rosemary, and salt. Knead until smooth.
3. Cover and let rise for 1 hour.
4. Preheat oven to 425°F (220°C). Spread dough on an oiled baking sheet.
5. Poke dimples into the dough, drizzle with olive oil, and sprinkle with sea salt.
6. Bake for 20-25 minutes until golden.

Baked Ziti with Chicken Sausage

Ingredients:

- 12 oz ziti pasta
- 1 lb chicken sausage, sliced
- 2 cups marinara sauce
- 1 cup ricotta cheese
- 1 cup shredded mozzarella cheese
- 1/4 cup grated Parmesan cheese
- 1 teaspoon Italian seasoning

Instructions:

1. Preheat oven to 375°F (190°C). Cook ziti until al dente.
2. Brown chicken sausage in a skillet. Mix with marinara sauce.
3. Combine ziti, ricotta, half the mozzarella, and sauce mixture in a baking dish.
4. Top with remaining mozzarella and Parmesan.
5. Bake for 20-25 minutes until bubbly and golden.

Pistachio Pesto Pasta

Ingredients:

- 12 oz pasta of choice
- 1/2 cup shelled pistachios
- 2 cups fresh basil leaves
- 1/4 cup grated Parmesan cheese
- 1/4 cup olive oil
- 2 cloves garlic
- **Salt and pepper**, to taste

Instructions:

1. Cook pasta according to package instructions.
2. Blend pistachios, basil, Parmesan, olive oil, garlic, salt, and pepper in a food processor.
3. Toss cooked pasta with the pesto. Adjust seasoning and serve.

Cabbage and Sausage Risotto

Ingredients:

- 1 cup Arborio rice
- 1/2 lb sausage, crumbled
- 1 cup shredded cabbage
- 1 small onion, diced
- 3 cups chicken broth, warmed
- 1/4 cup white wine
- 1/4 cup grated Parmesan cheese

Instructions:

1. Brown sausage in a pan. Add onion and sauté until translucent.
2. Stir in rice and cook for 1 minute. Add wine and let it absorb.
3. Gradually add broth, stirring, until rice is creamy and cooked.
4. Stir in cabbage and cook for 2 minutes. Finish with Parmesan.

Cacciatore with Cauliflower Rice

Ingredients:

- 4 chicken thighs
- 1 bell pepper, sliced
- 1 cup mushrooms, sliced
- 1 cup marinara sauce
- 1/2 cup chicken broth
- 1/4 cup olives
- 2 cups cauliflower rice
- 1 tablespoon olive oil

Instructions:

1. Sear chicken thighs in olive oil until golden. Remove and set aside.
2. Sauté bell peppers and mushrooms until softened.
3. Add marinara, broth, and olives. Simmer and return chicken to the pan.
4. Cook for 20-25 minutes until chicken is tender. Serve over cauliflower rice.

Baked Eggplant with Tomato and Basil

Ingredients:

- 2 large eggplants, sliced
- 1 cup marinara sauce
- 1/2 cup shredded mozzarella
- 1/4 cup grated Parmesan
- Fresh basil leaves

Instructions:

1. Preheat oven to 375°F (190°C). Roast eggplant slices for 10 minutes.
2. Layer eggplant, marinara, mozzarella, and Parmesan in a baking dish.
3. Bake for 20 minutes. Garnish with basil before serving.

Saffron Risotto with Scallops

Ingredients:

- **1 cup Arborio rice**
- **1/4 teaspoon saffron threads**, soaked in 2 tablespoons warm water
- **4 cups chicken broth**, warmed
- **1/4 cup white wine**
- **1/4 cup grated Parmesan cheese**
- **1 tablespoon butter**
- **8 large scallops**
- **1 tablespoon olive oil**

Instructions:

1. Cook rice in butter, adding wine and saffron water. Gradually add broth, stirring constantly.
2. Cook until rice is creamy. Stir in Parmesan and season.
3. Sear scallops in olive oil for 2-3 minutes per side. Serve atop risotto.

Grilled Shrimp and Zucchini Skewers

Ingredients:

- **1 lb large shrimp**, peeled and deveined
- **2 zucchinis**, sliced into rounds
- **2 tablespoons olive oil**
- **1 teaspoon garlic powder**
- **Salt and pepper**, to taste

Instructions:

1. Toss shrimp and zucchini with olive oil, garlic powder, salt, and pepper.
2. Thread onto skewers and grill for 3-4 minutes per side.

Lemon-Basil Chicken with Spaghetti

Ingredients:

- **4 chicken breasts**
- **1 lemon**, juiced and zested
- **2 tablespoons fresh basil**, chopped
- **2 tablespoons olive oil**
- **12 oz spaghetti**

Instructions:

1. Cook spaghetti and set aside.
2. Sear chicken in olive oil until golden. Remove and keep warm.
3. Deglaze pan with lemon juice, add zest and basil. Return chicken and toss with spaghetti.

Mushroom and Ricotta Stuffed Shells

Ingredients:

- **12 large pasta shells**
- **1 cup ricotta cheese**
- **1/2 cup Parmesan cheese**, grated
- **1 cup mushrooms**, finely chopped
- **1 clove garlic**, minced
- **1 cup marinara sauce**
- **1 tablespoon olive oil**
- **Salt and pepper**, to taste

Instructions:

1. Preheat oven to 375°F (190°C). Cook pasta shells until al dente.
2. Sauté mushrooms and garlic in olive oil. Let cool and mix with ricotta, Parmesan, salt, and pepper.
3. Stuff shells with the mixture and arrange in a baking dish with marinara sauce.
4. Bake for 20 minutes until heated through.

Fettuccine Alfredo with Cauliflower

Ingredients:

- **12 oz fettuccine**
- **2 cups cauliflower florets**
- **1/2 cup milk (or plant-based alternative)**
- **1/4 cup Parmesan cheese**, grated
- **2 cloves garlic**, minced
- **1 tablespoon butter**
- **Salt and pepper**, to taste

Instructions:

1. Cook fettuccine until al dente.
2. Steam cauliflower until tender, then blend with milk, garlic, Parmesan, and butter until smooth.
3. Toss pasta with the cauliflower Alfredo sauce. Adjust seasoning before serving.

Roasted Red Pepper Pappardelle

Ingredients:

- **12 oz pappardelle**
- **2 roasted red peppers**, peeled and seeded
- **1/2 cup heavy cream**
- **1/4 cup Parmesan cheese**, grated
- **1 tablespoon olive oil**
- **2 cloves garlic**, minced
- **Salt and pepper**, to taste

Instructions:

1. Blend roasted red peppers, cream, and Parmesan into a smooth sauce.
2. Cook pasta until al dente. In a pan, sauté garlic in olive oil.
3. Add the pepper sauce and simmer for 5 minutes. Toss with pasta and serve.

Polenta Fries with Marinara Sauce

Ingredients:

- **2 cups cooked polenta**, chilled and firm
- **2 tablespoons olive oil**
- **1 teaspoon garlic powder**
- **1 cup marinara sauce**, for dipping
- **Salt and pepper**, to taste

Instructions:

1. Preheat oven to 425°F (220°C). Slice polenta into fry shapes.
2. Toss with olive oil, garlic powder, salt, and pepper. Arrange on a baking sheet.
3. Bake for 25-30 minutes, turning halfway, until crispy. Serve with marinara sauce.

Spinach and Ricotta Tortellini

Ingredients:

- **12 oz tortellini pasta**, filled with spinach and ricotta
- **2 tablespoons butter**
- **2 cloves garlic**, minced
- **1/4 cup Parmesan cheese**, grated
- **1/4 cup heavy cream**
- **Salt and pepper**, to taste

Instructions:

1. Cook tortellini according to package instructions.
2. In a pan, melt butter and sauté garlic. Add cream and Parmesan, stirring until smooth.
3. Toss tortellini in the sauce and serve.

Lemon and Garlic Roasted Chicken

Ingredients:

- **4 chicken thighs**
- **1 lemon**, sliced
- **2 cloves garlic**, minced
- **2 tablespoons olive oil**
- **1 teaspoon fresh thyme**
- **Salt and pepper**, to taste

Instructions:

1. Preheat oven to 400°F (200°C). Arrange chicken thighs in a baking dish.
2. Rub with olive oil, garlic, thyme, salt, and pepper. Top with lemon slices.
3. Roast for 35-40 minutes until golden and cooked through.

Beetroot Ravioli with Goat Cheese

Ingredients:

- **1 package fresh pasta sheets**
- **1 cup cooked beetroot**, mashed
- **1/2 cup goat cheese**
- **1/4 cup ricotta cheese**
- **Salt and pepper**, to taste
- **1/4 cup butter**, for serving
- **1 tablespoon fresh sage**, chopped

Instructions:

1. Mix beetroot, goat cheese, ricotta, salt, and pepper for the filling.
2. Cut pasta sheets into squares, place filling, and seal into ravioli.
3. Cook in boiling water for 3-4 minutes. Toss with butter and sage.

Pumpkin Risotto with Sage

Ingredients:

- **1 cup Arborio rice**
- **1/2 cup pumpkin purée**
- **3 cups chicken or vegetable broth**, warmed
- **1/4 cup white wine**
- **1/4 cup Parmesan cheese**
- **1 tablespoon butter**
- **1 teaspoon fresh sage**, chopped

Instructions:

1. In a pan, toast rice in butter. Add wine and let absorb.
2. Gradually add broth, stirring, until rice is creamy and cooked.
3. Stir in pumpkin purée, Parmesan, and sage. Serve warm.

Grilled Veal Milanese

Ingredients:

- 4 veal cutlets
- 1/2 cup breadcrumbs
- 1/4 cup grated Parmesan cheese
- 2 eggs, beaten
- 1/4 cup olive oil
- **Salt and pepper**, to taste
- **Lemon wedges**, for serving

Instructions:

1. Coat veal cutlets in beaten egg, then breadcrumbs mixed with Parmesan.
2. Heat olive oil in a skillet and cook cutlets until golden, about 3 minutes per side.
3. Serve with lemon wedges for garnish.

Spinach and Mushroom Stuffed Peppers

Ingredients:

- **4 bell peppers**, halved and seeds removed
- **2 cups spinach**, chopped
- **1 cup mushrooms**, diced
- **1/2 cup cooked quinoa or rice**
- **1/4 cup Parmesan cheese**, grated
- **1/4 cup mozzarella cheese**, shredded
- **1 clove garlic**, minced
- **1 tablespoon olive oil**
- **Salt and pepper**, to taste

Instructions:

1. Preheat oven to 375°F (190°C). Arrange bell peppers in a baking dish.
2. Heat olive oil in a skillet, sauté garlic, mushrooms, and spinach until softened.
3. Mix the sautéed vegetables with quinoa, Parmesan, salt, and pepper.
4. Stuff the peppers with the mixture and top with mozzarella.
5. Bake for 25-30 minutes until the peppers are tender and the cheese is melted.

Roasted Tomato and Basil Soup

Ingredients:

- **6 large tomatoes**, halved
- **1 small onion**, chopped
- **3 cloves garlic**, peeled
- **2 cups vegetable broth**
- **1/4 cup fresh basil leaves**
- **2 tablespoons olive oil**
- **Salt and pepper**, to taste

Instructions:

1. Preheat oven to 400°F (200°C). Arrange tomatoes and garlic on a baking sheet, drizzle with olive oil, and roast for 20-25 minutes.
2. In a pot, sauté onion until softened. Add the roasted tomatoes and garlic.
3. Pour in vegetable broth and simmer for 10 minutes.
4. Blend the soup with fresh basil until smooth. Adjust seasoning and serve warm.

Baked Parmesan-Crusted Zucchini

Ingredients:

- **2 medium zucchinis**, sliced into sticks
- **1/2 cup breadcrumbs**
- **1/4 cup Parmesan cheese**, grated
- **1 teaspoon garlic powder**
- **1 egg**, beaten
- **Salt and pepper**, to taste

Instructions:

1. Preheat oven to 425°F (220°C). Line a baking sheet with parchment paper.
2. Mix breadcrumbs, Parmesan, garlic powder, salt, and pepper.
3. Dip zucchini sticks in egg, then coat with the breadcrumb mixture.
4. Arrange on the baking sheet and bake for 20-25 minutes until golden and crisp.

Tuna Puttanesca

Ingredients:

- **12 oz spaghetti**
- **1 can tuna**, drained
- **1/4 cup black olives**, sliced
- **2 tablespoons capers**
- **2 cups canned diced tomatoes**
- **2 cloves garlic**, minced
- **2 tablespoons olive oil**
- **1/4 teaspoon red pepper flakes** (optional)
- **Salt and pepper**, to taste

Instructions:

1. Cook spaghetti until al dente.
2. Heat olive oil in a skillet and sauté garlic until fragrant. Add tomatoes, olives, capers, and red pepper flakes. Simmer for 10 minutes.
3. Stir in tuna and cook until heated through. Toss with spaghetti and serve.

Gnocchi with Brown Butter Sage Sauce

Ingredients:

- **1 pound potato gnocchi** (store-bought or homemade)
- **1/4 cup unsalted butter**
- **6 fresh sage leaves**
- **1/4 cup Parmesan cheese**, grated
- **Salt and pepper**, to taste

Instructions:

1. Cook gnocchi in boiling water until they float. Drain and set aside.
2. In a skillet, melt butter over medium heat. Add sage leaves and cook until the butter browns and the sage is crispy.
3. Toss the cooked gnocchi in the brown butter sauce. Serve with Parmesan and freshly ground pepper.

www.ingramcontent.com/pod-product-compliance
Lightning Source LLC
LaVergne TN
LVHW081339060526
838201LV00055B/2752